THE UNOFFICIAL BIG GREEN EGG COOKBOOK

COMPLETE SMOKER COOKBOOK FOR REAL PITMASTERS, THE ULTIMATE GUIDE FOR SMOKING MEAT, FISH, GAME AND VEGETABLES

DANIEL MURRAY

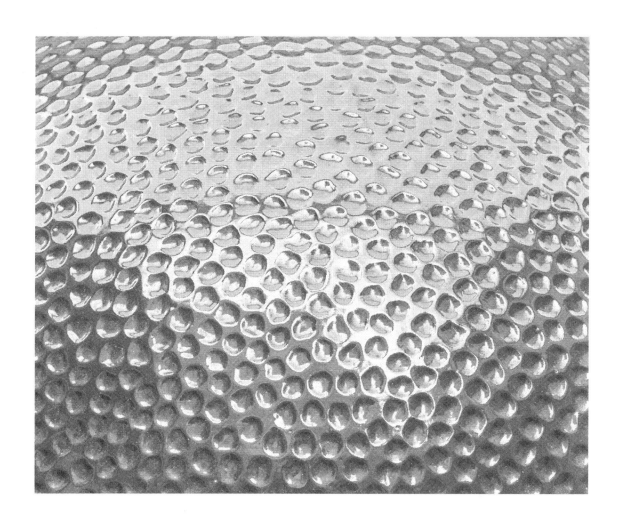

TABLE OF CONTENTS

AN INTRODUCTION TO SMOKED FOOD

Through history, smoking been a preferred way of preserving food, but it so much more than just a way to keep food from going bad! Smoking also introduces complex and delicious flavors into dishes that are otherwise often bland or uninteresting. In modern cooking, it's a great way to mix up staples in your home cooking, and it can be a really fantastic way to wow people at a potluck, or to host an incredible dinner party. Smoking is not

only inventive and delicious, it also makes it really easy to make large quantities of food at the same time without too much fuss. Traditionally, smoking is done by burning wood chips in a small enclosed area with the food, allowing the food to be cooked very slowly, while absorbing the rich smoky flavor. Today, smoking is often associated with sports tail-gaiting parties and small family get-togethers. This guide is designed to both embrace that culture, and also offer up some techniques and recipes that will let you take your smoking to the next level: full-blown gourmet food full of layered and nuanced deliciousness.

While Masterbuilt may not be the oldest Smoker manufacturer out there in the market, they are still around from the 1970s and knows what they are doing! Masterbuilt is a long-standing brand that has accumulated a vast reputation for being one of the top Smoker Manufacturers out there with a company that was built on faith, family and sheer hard work! This is a company that always tries to combine invention, faith and family values and tries to come up with appliances that are both robust in features and extremely easy to use for beginners. If you are reading this book, then you are probably either deciding to buy a Masterbuilt Smoker or already have purchased one and are looking for amazing recipes to explore! If you are from the latter group, you may skip the intro and jump right into the recipes! However, if you are new to Smoking, then I would highly encourage you to go through this brief yet useful introductory chapter. Throughout the following pages, I will give you an overview of Smoking and let you know how to use and adequately take care of your Masterbuilt Electric Smoker (Alongside a brief buying guide)!

CHAPTER 1: BEEF RECIPES

HEARTY COFFEE RUBBED BEEF ROAST

SERVING: 4

PREP TIME: 60 MINUTES +24 HOURS

COOK TIME: 1 AND 1/2 HOURS

RECOMMENDED WOOD TYPE: HICKORY WOOD

INGREDIENTS

- 4 pounds beef chuck roast
- Olive oil
- Salt and pepper to taste
- Salted butter, melted

THE RUB

- 1 tablespoons onion powder
- 2 tablespoons smoked paprika
- 1 tablespoon garlic powder
- 1 teaspoon chili powder
- 1 teaspoon mustard powder
- 1 teaspoon oregano
- 1 teaspoon coriander
- 1 teaspoon white sugar
- 1 teaspoon dried thyme
- 1 tablespoon salt
- 2 tablespoons brown sugar
- ¾ cup ground coffee

HOW TO

1. Prepare the rub by mixing all of the listed ingredients in a small sized bowl
2. Brush the roast with the mixture all over with oil and season with pepper
3. Cover well with the rub and let it chill for 24 hours
4. Let the meat come for room temperature
5. Pre-heat your EGG to 275 degrees F and set it for direct cooking
6. Arrange meat on one side of your grill and cook for 1 and ½ hours until internal temperature reaches 125 degrees F
7. Bate with butter and tent with foil, let it sit for 30 minutes more
8. Slice and serve, enjoy!

NUTRITION VALUES (PER SERVING)

- Calories: 397
- Fat: 12g
- Carbohydrates: 31g
- Protein: 40g

BOURBON BEEF BURGERS

SERVING: 4

PREP TIME: 10 MINUTES

COOK TIME: 10 MINUTES

RECOMMENDED WOOD TYPE: HICKORY WOOD

INGREDIENTS

- 1 pound ground beef

THE RUB

- 2 tablespoons onion soup mix
- 2 tablespoons Worcestershire sauce
- 2 tablespoons bourbon
- 1 teaspoon hot sauce
- 4 brioche buns, toasted

HOW TO

1. Take a large bowl and mix all ingredients under rubbing alongside beef
2. Shape the meat 4 equally sized patties and make an indent
3. Pre-heat your smoker 375 degrees F and set it to direct cooking
4. Place directly on grill and cook for 5 minutes on each side until medium-rare
5. Serve burgers inside buns and enjoy!

NUTRITION VALUES (PER SERVING)

- Calories: 639
- Fat: 19g
- Carbohydrates: 90g
- Protein: 27g

BUTTERED UP PRIME FRESH RIB

SERVING: 4

PREP TIME: 30 MINUTES

COOK TIME: 120 MINUTES

RECOMMENDED WOOD TYPE: HICKORY WOOD

INGREDIENTS

- 5 pounds boneless rib-eye roast
- Salt and pepper

THE RUB

- 1 cup butter
- ¼ cup fresh thyme chopped
- 4 garlic cloves, peeled and crushed
- ¼ cup fresh parsley, chopped
- ¼ cup fresh tarragon, chopped

HOW TO

1. Season beef with salt and pepper
2. Prepare mixture by taking a small bowl and mixing all the rub ingredients, spread mixture all over beef
3. Pre-heat your EGG to 325 degrees F and set it indirect cooking
4. Place beef on grate and cook for 1 and ½ -2 hours until meat shows an internal temperature of 125 degrees F
5. Transfer cooked meat to serving platter and place a tent, set it for 15-20 minutes
6. Slice thickly and enjoy!

NUTRITION VALUES (PER SERVING)

- Calories: 1332
- Fat: 95g
- Carbohydrates: 12g
- Protein: 87g

BEER BEEF RIBS

SERVING: 4

PREP TIME: 60 MINUTES

COOK TIME: 5-6 HOURS

RECOMMENDED WOOD TYPE: OAK WOOD

INGREDIENTS

- 1 rack beef short ribs

THE RUB

- Olive oil
- Salt and pepper to taste
- 1 tablespoon garlic powder
- 1 bottle stout beer

HOW TO

1. Peel away membrane from the bone side of your ribs
2. Brush rack with olive oil and season with salt, pepper and garlic
3. Pre-heat your EGG to 265 degrees F
4. Arrange ribs on grate (bone side facing down) and grill for a few hours, flip and cook until both sides have a rich gold brown texture
5. Transfer to disposable aluminum foil and pour over stout beer, secure with foil and transfer back to grill
6. Cook for few hours more until internal temperature reaches 200 degrees F
7. Cut rack into individual bones and enjoy!

NUTRITION VALUES (PER SERVING)

- Calories: 392
- Fat: 34g
- Carbohydrates: 2g
- Protein: 18g

INDIAN COOL KEBAB

SERVING: 4

PREP TIME: 20 MINUTES + 4-8 HOURS MARINATING TIME

COOK TIME: 40-60 MINUTES

RECOMMENDED WOOD TYPE: OAK WOOD

INGREDIENTS

- 1 pound beef tenderloin, cut into 1 inch cubes
- 2 pounds strip steak, cut into 1 inch cubes
- 1 large onion, cut into 1 inch cubes
- 1 bell pepper, cut into 1 inch cubes
- 1 zucchini, cut into 1 inch cubes
- 10 ounces cherry tomatoes
- ¼ cup olive oil
- ½ cup steak seasoning

How To

1. Take a large sized bowl and add tenderloin, strip steak, onion, zucchini, bell pepper, tomatoes and mix well with olive oil
2. Season with steak seasoning and stir well, let it marinate for 4-8 hours
3. Pre-heat your EGG to 225 degrees F and set it for direct cooking
4. Make kebabs by skewering the meat and veggies alternatively, place in your EGG and smoke for 45 minutes
5. Once the internal temperature reaches 135 degrees F, serve and enjoy!

Nutrition Values (Per Serving)

- Calories: 559
- Fat: 5g
- Carbohydrates: 57g
- Protein: 25g

CHAPTER 2: PORK RECIPES

COOL PORK BUTT

SERVING: 4

PREP TIME: 2 HOURS + 4 HOURS SOAK TIME

COOK TIME: 6-10 HOURS

RECOMMENDED WOOD TYPE: PECAN WOOD

INGREDIENTS

- 7 pounds pork butt roast
- 2 tablespoons ground New Mexico Chile Powder
- 4 tablespoons packed brown sugar

HOW TO

1. Soak your pork butter in brine solution for 4 hours
2. Make sure to cover the butt before placing in your fridge
3. Pre-heat your EGG to 225 degrees F and set it for indirect cooking
4. Take a small bowl and add chili powder, brown sugar alongside any other seasoning that you may fancy
5. Rub butt with your mixture
6. Take the butt and transfer to your EGG, place dripping pan
7. Smoke for 6-10 hours , the internal temperature should reach 100 degrees F

NUTRITION VALUES (PER SERVING)

- Calories: 326
- Fat: 4g
- Carbohydrates: 4g
- Protein: 40

BURNT UP PORK BELLY

SERVING: 4

PREP TIME: 10 MINUTES

COOK TIME: 4 HOURS

RECOMMENDED WOOD TYPE: HICKORY WOOD

INGREDIENTS

- 1 pound pork belly
- BBQ rub of your choice
- BBQ sauce of your choice
- Honey as needed
- Apple juice as neeeded

How To

1. Pre-heat your EGG to 275 degrees F and set it for indirect cooking
2. Trim the pork belly and cut it up into 1 inch sized cubes
3. Generously season the pork belly with BBQ rub and transfer them to your EGG
4. Smoke for about 3 hours, making sure to keep spraying them with apple juice after every hour
5. Once the internal temperature reaches 190 degrees F , remove the pork from your EGG and transfer to a aluminum foiled pan
6. Toss with evenly drizzled BBQ sauce
7. Drizzle more honey on top and transfer the foiled pan (with meat) back to the EGG
8. Cook for 1 hour more until everything is caramelized
9. Serve and enjoy!

Nutrition Values (Per Serving)

- Calories: 518
- Fat: 53g
- Carbohydrates: 10g
- Protein: 9g

PLUM GLAZED PORK BELLY KEBABS

SERVING: 3

PREP TIME: 10 MINUTES

COOK TIME: 25 MINUTES

RECOMMENDED WOOD TYPE: HICKORY WOOD

INGREDIENTS

- 1 pound pork belly
- ½ cup Asia plum sauce
- 2 teaspoons Asian chili paste
- 1 tablespoon soy sauce
- 2 garlic clove, minced
- Salt to taste
- Pepper to taste
- 8 skewers

HOW TO

1. Cut pork belly into cubes of 1 inch thickness, thread onto skewers and season with salt and pepper
2. Make plum glaze by taking a medium sized bowl and adding Asian plum sauce, chili paste, soy sauce, garlic and mix
3. Pre-heat your EGG to 350 degrees F and set it to direct cooking
4. Place kebab threaded skewers on grid and cook for 25 minutes, making sure to turn occasionally
5. Make sure to baste for just 10 minutes before cooking completes, make sure to not burn it
6. Once turn, remove from grill and serve
7. Enjoy!

NUTRITION VALUES (PER SERVING)

- Calories: 135
- Fat: 9g
- Carbohydrates: 5g
- Protein: 17g

CEDAR PLANK PORK CHOPS

SERVING: 4

PREP TIME: 5 HOURS

COOK TIME: 15-20 MINUTES

RECOMMENDED WOOD TYPE: OAK WOOD

INGREDIENTS

- 2 big green egg cedar planks, soaked up
- Fresh pieces of bay leaves
- Your favorite JAVA rub
- 1 chicken bouillon cube
- ½ cup chicken marinade of your choosing
- ¾ cup of canola oil
- 4 pork chops, double bone- in

HOW TO

1. Soak the planks for about 2 hours prior to your grilling session
2. Take a bowl and add oil, marinade, cube and blend for 45 seconds
3. Transfer pork chops to a pan and pour oil over chops
4. Top them up with leaves
5. Turn chops over, making sure that they are fully coated
6. Let them sit for 3-4 hours
7. Remove from marinade and drain them well
8. Season both sides thoroughly
9. Pre-heat your EGG to 400 degrees F
10. Transfer soaked up planks on EGG and heat them for 30 seconds
11. Flip and add seasoned chops to the plank
12. Cook for about 15-20 minutes until the internal temperature reaches 145 degrees F
13. Serve and enjoy!

NUTRITION VALUES (PER SERVING)

- Calories: 118
- Fat: 7g
- Carbohydrates: 5g
- Protein: 13g

HERBED UP PORK RIBS

SERVING: 4
PREP TIME: 1 HOUR
COOK TIME: 30 – 60 MINUTES
RECOMMENDED WOOD TYPE: PECAN WOOD

INGREDIENTS

- 3-4 pounds pork short ribs
- ½ cup Dijon mustard
- 6 tablespoons rosemary, dried
- ½ cup thyme, dried
- 2 tablespoons oregano, dried

- 2 tablespoons salt
- 1 tablespoon pepper
- ¾ cup honey
- 10 garlic cloves
- 3 lemons, juiced

How To

1. Take a mortar and pestle and add garlic, pepper, herbs and salt
2. Mash well to form a paste
3. Rub the ribs with the mustard, making sure to cover all sides
4. Let them sit for 45 minutes
5. Take a small sized bowl and add lemon juice, honey
6. Pre-heat your EGG to 325 degrees F and bring the set it for indirect cooking
7. Transfer ribs to opposite side of your charcoal and cook them until the internal temperature reaches 180 degrees F
8. Brush with the honey mix
9. Remove ribs once the internal temperature reaches 195 degrees F
10. Brush with more lemon and honey
11. Let them rest for 15 minutes
12. Enjoy!

Nutrition Values (Per Serving)

- Calories: 100
- Fat: 2g
- Carbohydrates: 2g
- Protein: 18g

CHAPTER 3: LAMB RECIPES

GARLIC AND HERBED LAMB RACK

SERVING: 4

PREP TIME: 10 MINUTES + 15 MINUTES

COOK TIME: 5-10 MINUTES

RECOMMENDED WOOD TYPE: HICKORY WOOD

INGREDIENTS

- 2 racks lamb

THE RUB

- ½ bunch fresh rosemary, needles removed
- ½ bunch fresh thyme leaves, chopped
- 6 garlic cloves, peeled and minced
- Salt and pepper to taste
- Mustard as needed

HOW TO

1. Add the rub ingredients in a bowl
2. Brush a thin layer of mustard over racks and coat with herb mixture
3. Pre-heat your EGG to 355 degrees F and set it for direct cooking
4. Arrange lamb on grill and lock lid, cook for 8 minutes, making sure to turn after ever y 2 minutes
5. Let the lamb cook for 15 minutes more until the internal temperature reaches 120 degrees F
6. Take lamb racks off the grill and make a foil tent, let it rest for a few minutes
7. Slice and serve
8. Enjoy!

NUTRITION VALUES (PER SERVING)

- Calories: 903
- Fat: 83g
- Carbohydrates: 5g
- Protein: 34g

MEDI-LAMB AND FETA BURGERS

SERVING: 4

PREP TIME: 10 MINUTES

COOK TIME: 5-10 MINUTES

RECOMMENDED WOOD TYPE: HICKORY WOOD

INGREDIENTS

- 2 pounds ground lamb
- 1 pound ground beef

THE RUB

- ½ cup feta, crumbled
- 1 tablespoon BBQ rub
- 4 brioche buns, toasted

HOW TO

1. Add ground meat, feta, BBQ rub in a bowl and mix well
2. Use hands to prepare 4 patties
3. Pre-heat your EGG to 500 degrees F
4. Arrange patties on grill and cook for a few minutes each side, close vents and smoke for 5 minutes
5. Let the patties rest and serve in buns
6. Enjoy!

NUTRITION VALUES (PER SERVING)

- Calories: 254
- Fat: 18g
- Carbohydrates: 12g
- Protein: 12g

RUBBED UP SAGE LAMB CHOPS

SERVING: 4

PREP TIME: 10 MINUTES + OVERNIGHT COOL

COOK TIME: 20-30 MINUTES

RECOMMENDED WOOD TYPE: HICKORY WOOD

INGREDIENTS

- 2 pounds lamb rib chops

The Rub

- 8 ounces fresh sage
- 2 garlic cloves
- 4 sprigs thyme
- 6 tablespoons olive oil
- Pinch of salt and pepper to taste
- Butter as needed

How To

1. Crush sage to release oil
2. Place sage, garlic, thyme in a large bowl and add meat, drizzle olive oil on top an season with salt and pepper
3. Toss well to combine
4. Cover tightly with plastic wrap and let it chill overnight
5. Pre-heat your EGG to 300 degrees F
6. Transfer lamb to a skillet and add a knob of butter
7. Baste with more butter and cook until medium rare and internal temperature is 120 degrees F
8. Let it rest for a few minutes and serve, enjoy!

Nutrition Values (Per Serving)

- Calories: 459
- Fat: 32g
- Carbohydrates: 13g
- Protein: 21g

CHAPTER 4: POULTRY RECIPES

GREEK HERBED ROASTED CHICKEN

SERVING: 4

PREP TIME: 10 MINUTES + 60 MINUTES

COOK TIME: 20-30 MINUTES

RECOMMENDED WOOD TYPE: HICKORY WOOD

INGREDIENTS

- 3 and ½ pounds roasting chicken

THE RUB

- ¼ cup water
- 2 chicken stock cubes
- ½ cup fresh lemon juice
- 1 tablespoon lemon pepper seasoning
- ½ cup canola oil seasoning
- 1 tablespoon dried oregano
- Zest of 1 lemon
- ¼ cup fresh parsley, chopped
- Chicken stock

How To

1. Prepare the seasoning by mixing all the ingredients in a bowl and blending it using an immersion blender
2. Place chicken in a stainless steel bowl and pour marinade, let it chill for 4 hours, making sure turn it a few times
3. Take chicken out and drip excess
4. Pre-heat your EGG to 350 degrees F
5. Arrange chicken on vertical roasted and fill with beer/chicken stock
6. Arrange vertical roaster inside a roasting tin to catch any dripping
7. Arrange on the cooking grid
8. Cook until the internal temperature reaches 165 degrees F
9. Serve and enjoy!

NUTRITION VALUES (PER SERVING)

- Calories: 847
- Fat: 44g
- Carbohydrates: 47g
- Protein: 61g

RANCH-ROSEMARY CHICKEN KEBABS

SERVING: 4

PREP TIME: 10 MINUTES +30 MINUTES

COOK TIME: 10 MINUTES

RECOMMENDED WOOD TYPE: HICKORY WOOD

INGREDIENTS

- 5 boneless, skinless chicken breasts, cubed

THE RUB

- ½ cup ranch dressing
- ½ cup olive oil
- 1 tablespoon fresh rosemary, minced
- 3 tablespoons Worcestershire sauce
- 1 teaspoon lemon juice
- 2 teaspoons salt
- ¼ teaspoon pepper
- 1 teaspoon white vinegar
- 1 tablespoon sugar

HOW TO

1. Prepare marinade by adding ranch dressing, olive oil, rosemary, sauce, lemon juice, salt, vinegar, sugar in a bowl and mix well
2. Let it stand for a while
3. Add chicken and toss well, let it chill for 30 minutes
4. Thread cubes onto skewers and arrange on a lightly oiled grid
5. Pre-heat your EGG to 400 degrees F and set it for direct cooking
6. Grill for 10 minutes until cook well
7. Enjoy!

NUTRITION VALUES (PER SERVING)

- Calories: 408
- Fat: 20g
- Carbohydrates: 18g
- Protein: 38g

COOL TURKEY PARMIGIANA

SERVING: 4

PREP TIME: 20 MINUTES

COOK TIME: 30 MINUTES

RECOMMENDED WOOD TYPE: HICKORY WOOD

INGREDIENTS

- 1 pound turkey breast fillets, boneless

The Rub

- 2 egg whites
- 1 tablespoon water
- 2 tablespoons Italian seasoned breadcrumbs
- 2 tablespoons parmesan cheese
- 1 cup marinara sauce
- 1 cup mozzarella sauce, shredded

How To

1. Whisk in egg whites and water in a shallow dish, take another dish and add breadcrumbs and parmesan
2. Dip each turkey fillet first in egg whites and then in bread crumbs
3. Arrange meat in pan and place on cooking
4. Pre-heat your EGG to 400 degrees F and set it for in-direct cooking
5. Cook for 30 minutes, pour marinara sauce over breaded turkey and sprinkle over mozzarella
6. Cook for 5 minutes more until cheese melts
7. Enjoy!

Nutrition Values (Per Serving)

- Calories: 313
- Fat: 23g
- Carbohydrates: 5g
- Protein: 22g

PARMESAN CHICKEN LEGS

SERVING: 4

PREP TIME: 10 MINUTES

COOK TIME: 20-40 MINUTES

RECOMMENDED WOOD TYPE: HICKORY WOOD

INGREDIENTS

- ½ cup parmesan cheese
- 3 tablespoons garlic powder
- ½ cup butter, melted
- ½ cup chicken wing rub, your choice
- 6 chicken legs

How To

1. Pre-heat your EGG to 375 degrees F
2. Season chicken legs with wing rub, mix in butter and garlic well
3. Add chicken to EGG, keep cooking until the internal temperature is 165 degrees F , making sure to flip it after every 5 minutes
4. Remove and transfer to Iron Skillet
5. Sprinkle parmesan cheese and cook for 10-15 minutes more until the cheese melts completely
6. Enjoy!

Nutrition Values (Per Serving)

- Calories: 932
- Fat: 66g
- Carbohydrates: 24g
- Protein: 62g

ROUGH CHICKEN MEATBALLS

SERVING: 4

PREP TIME: 10 MINUTES

COOK TIME: 20-30 MINUTES

RECOMMENDED WOOD TYPE: HICKORY WOOD

INGREDIENTS

- Blue cheese for serving
- 2 tablespoons butter, melted
- 1 pound lean ground chicken
- 1 large egg, white
- 1 teaspoon garlic, minced
- ¼ cup red onion, chopped
- ¼ cup celery, chopped
- 1/3 cup hot sauce
- ¾ cup panko bread crumbs

HOW TO

1. Pre-heat your EGG to 400 degrees F
2. Take a bowl and add panko, sauce, red onion, celery, garlic, egg white and chicken
3. Mix well and form the batter into small balls
4. Grease the inner part of your EGG's drip pan and add meatballs to pan, lock dome and bake for 20 minutes
5. Take a bowl and mix ½ cup sauce and add melted butter, add meatballs and serve with blue cheese dressing

NUTRITION VALUES (PER SERVING)

- Calories: 231
- Fat: 10g
- Carbohydrates: 6g
- Protein: 27g

CHICKEN WINGS

SERVING: 4

PREP TIME: 10 MINUTES

COOK TIME: 20-30 MINUTES

RECOMMENDED WOOD TYPE: APPLE WOOD

INGREDIENTS

- 1 pound chicken wings
- 1 tablespoon vegetable oil
- 1 cup onion sriracha BBQ sauce
- 2 tablespoons smoke and sweet seasoning

How To

1. Pre-heat your EGG to 350 degrees F
2. Drizzle wings with oil and add seasoning, toss well
3. Add seasoned wings to EGG and close dome, cook for about 30 minutes, flip and cook for 20 minutes more
4. Remove EGG
5. Increase the temperature to 400 degrees F
6. Coat wings with Onion Sriracha Sauce, transfer them back to EGG and cook for 5 minutes more until caramelized
7. Remove Wings and let them rest
8. Enjoy!

Nutrition Values (Per Serving)

- Calories: 169
- Fat: 15g
- Carbohydrates: 0g
- Protein: 8g

CHAPTER 5: VEGETABLES RECIPES

AWESOME SMOKED CABBAGE

SERVING: 4

PREP TIME: 10 MINUTES

COOK TIME: 120 MINUTES

RECOMMENDED WOOD TYPE: MAPLE WOOD

INGREDIENTS

- 1 head cabbage, cored
- 4 tablespoons butter
- 2 tablespoons bacon, rendered fat
- 1 chicken bouillon cube
- 1 teaspoon fresh ground black pepper
- 1 garlic clove, minced

HOW TO

1. Pre-heat your EGG to 240 degrees F
2. Core cabbage and add butter, cube, bacon fat, pepper and garlic to the hole
3. Wrap cabbage in foil about 2/3rds way up
4. Keep the top open
5. Transfer to Egg and smoke for 2 hours
6. Enjoy!

NUTRITION VALUES (PER SERVING)

- Calories: 231
- Fat: 10g
- Carbohydrates: 26g
- Protein: 10g

ROSEMARY POTATO WEDGES

SERVING: 4

PREP TIME: 10 MINUTES

COOK TIME: 90 MINUTES

RECOMMENDED WOOD TYPE: MAPLE WOOD

INGREDIENTS

- 4-6 large russet potatoes, cut into wedges
- ¼ cup olive oil
- 2 garlic cloves, minced
- 2 tablespoons rosemary leaves, chopped
- 2 teaspoons salt
- 1 teaspoon fresh ground pepper
- 1 teaspoon sugar
- 1 teaspoon onion powder

HOW TO

1. Pre-heat your EGG to 250 degrees F
2. Take a large bowl and add potatoes and olive oil, mix well
3. Take another small bowl and add garlic, salt, rosemary, pepper, sugar, onion powder and sprinkle on all sides of the wedges
4. Transfer to a rack and to your EGG
5. Smoke for 1 and ½ hours
6. Enjoy!

NUTRITION VALUES (PER SERVING)

- Calories: 291
- Fat: 10g
- Carbohydrates: 46g
- Protein: 5g

SMOKED UP MAC AND CHEESE

SERVING: 4

PREP TIME: 25 MINUTES

COOK TIME: 60 MINUTES

RECOMMENDED WOOD TYPE: HICKORY WOOD

INGREDIENTS

- 4 tablespoons butter
- 3 tablespoons all-purpose flour
- 3 cups whole milk
- 2 cups cheddar cheese, shredded
- 2 cups jack cheese, shredded
- 1 cup parmesan cheese, grated

54

- 8 ounces cream cheese, cubed
- 2 teaspoons salt
- 1 teaspoon fresh ground black pepper
- 1 pound elbow macaroni, cooked
- Cooking spray to taste

How To

1. Pre-heat your EGG to 225 degrees F
2. Take a large saucepan and place it over medium heat, add butter and let it heat p
3. Whisk in flour and whisk for 1 minute, slowly whisk in milk and bring mix to a boil
4. Lower heat to low and simmer for 5 minutes , remove heat
5. Add cheese and stir until cheese melts
6. Stir in pepper, salt and cooked macaroni
7. Spray an aluminum foil roasting pan with cooking spray and transfer the mac and cheese mix
8. Top with remaining cheese
9. Smoke for 1 hour until bubbly
10. Enjoy!

Nutrition Values (Per Serving)

- Calories: 183
- Fat: 11g
- Carbohydrates: 14g
- Protein:10g

SMOKED TOMATO AND MOZA DIP

SERVING: 4

PREP TIME: 5 MINUTES

COOK TIME: 60 MINUTES

RECOMMENDED WOOD TYPE: HICKORY WOOD

INGREDIENTS

- 8 ounces smoked mozzarella cheese, shredded
- 8 ounces Colby cheese, shredded
- ½ cup parmesan cheese, grated
- 1 cup sour cream
- 1 cup sun-dried tomatoes
- 1 and ½ teaspoon salt
- 1 teaspoon pepper
- 1 teaspoon dried basil
- 1 teaspoon dried oregano
- 1 teaspoon red pepper flakes
- 1 garlic clove, minced
- ½ teaspoon onion powder
- Fresh toast for serving

HOW TO

1. Pre-heat your EGG to 275 degrees F
2. Take a large bowl and stir in cheese, tomatoes, pepper, salt, basil, oregano, pepper flakes, garlic, onion powder and mix well
3. Transfer mix to a hard steel skillet and transfer to your EGG
4. Smoke for 1 hour
5. Serve and enjoy!

NUTRITION VALUES (PER SERVING)

- Calories: 174
- Fat: 11g
- Carbohydrates: 15g
- Protein: 10g

CHAPTER 6: FISH AND SEAFOOD RECIPES

HONEY AND PECAN HALIBUT

SERVING: 4

PREP TIME: 10 MINUTES

COOK TIME: 20-30 MINUTES

RECOMMENDED WOOD TYPE: HICKORY WOOD

INGREDIENTS

- 4 halibuts
- Pecan rub
- 4 tablespoons clover honey

THE RUB

- ½ cup salt
- 1 cup sugar
- 4 tablespoons cumin
- 1 tablespoon white pepper
- 2 bay leaves crushed
- 1 gallon water

HOW TO

1. Prepare bring by mixing in salt, sugar, cumin, white pepper, bay leaves, water and mix well
2. Pour bring over halibut fillets and keep it on the side for 2 hours
3. Remove halibut and transfer to kitchen towel, pat dry
4. Season both sides with pecan dry rub, skin side facing down
5. Pre-heat your EGG to 275 degrees F
6. Transfer to EGG skin side facing down, arrange fish fillets directly on cooking grate and smoke until internal temperature reaches 135 degrees F
7. Drizzle fish with warm honey just 10 minutes prior to completion of cooking
8. Serve and enjoy!

NUTRITION VALUES (PER SERVING)

- Calories: 246
- Fat: 9g
- Carbohydrates: 7g
- Protein: 33g

LEMON AND ROSEMARY GROUPER

SERVING: 4

PREP TIME: 10 MINUTES + 60 MINUTES

COOK TIME: 20-30 MINUTES

RECOMMENDED WOOD TYPE: HICKORY WOOD

INGREDIENTS

- 3 grouper fillets

The Rub

- 1 tablespoon freshly squeezed lemon juice
- ½ teaspoon of dried rosemary and crushed
- ½ teaspoons olive oil
- ¼ teaspoon salt
- Dash of black pepper

Saute

- ¼ cup tomato , seed and diced
- 1 teaspoon dried basil
- 1 tablespoon green onion, chopped
- 1 and ½ teaspoon wine vinegar
- ¼ teaspoon orange peel, grated

How To

1. Take a zip bag and add rosemary, fresh lemon juice, salt, pepper and olive oil
2. Add fish fillets to bag and seal bag
3. Transfer to fridge and let it chill for 60 minutes
4. Drain and discard marinade
5. Pre-heat your EGG to 350 degrees F and set it for DIRECT cooking
6. Transfer fish to grid and grill both sides until fish fillets flake easily using a fork
7. Take a pan and add sauce ingredients and mix well
8. Place over medium heat and heat it up
9. Serve fish fillets with sauce and enjoy!

Nutrition Values (Per Serving)

- Calories: 485
- Fat: 17g
- Carbohydrates: 35g
- Protein: 48g

COOL CEDAR-PLANKED SWEET CHILI SALMON

SERVING: 4

PREP TIME: 10 MINUTES

COOK TIME: 20-30 MINUTES

RECOMMENDED WOOD TYPE: HICKORY WOOD

INGREDIENTS

- Thai sweet chili sauce of your desire
- Sweet and smoky seasoning as you need
- 2 salmon fillets cut up nicely to fit on a plank

HOW TO

1. Pre-heat your EGG to 350 degrees F
2. Place planks in pan and cover with water, let them soak for 2 hours
3. Season the fillets with seasoning, pour Thai sauce to a pot sauce and gently warm
4. Place plank on your EGG's cooking grid, lock dome and let them heat for about 2 minutes
5. Use tongs to flip the planks and place salmon on plank
6. Coat with sauce and lock dome, let them cook for 20-25 minutes
7. Serve an enjoy!

NUTRITION VALUES (PER SERVING)

- Calories: 297
- Fat: 15g
- Carbohydrates: 20g
- Protein: 19g

CRAB CAKES WITH BBQ RANCH SAUCE

SERVING: 4

PREP TIME: 10 MINUTES + 60 MINUTES

COOK TIME: 20-30 MINUTES

RECOMMENDED WOOD TYPE: HICKORY WOOD

INGREDIENTS

- 1 pound lump crabmeat
- ½ cup BBQ sauce of your choice
- ½ cup ranch dressing

THE RUB

- 2 large eggs, beaten
- 2 jalapenos, seeded and minced
- ½ cup panko breadcrumbs
- ½ cup mayonnaise
- 1 tablespoon fresh parsley, chopped
- 2 teaspoons hot seasoning

HOW TO

1. Take a bowl and add eggs, jalapenos, breadcrumbs, mayonnaise, parsley and hot seasoning to a bowl, mix well
2. Add crab meat to mixture using clean hands gently combine
3. Form mixture into 4 evenly sized balls using palm and flatten them into patties
4. Pre-heat your EGG to 375 degrees F
5. Transfer to EGG and smoke for 18-20 minutes
6. Take a bowl and mix in BBQ sauce, ranch dressing and serve the sauce
7. Enjoy!

NUTRITION VALUES (PER SERVING)

- Calories: 456
- Fat: 27g
- Carbohydrates: 26g
- Protein: 27g

HONEY AND PLANKED SALMON

SERVING: 4

PREP TIME: 10 MINUTES + 60 MINUTES

COOK TIME: 20-25 MINUTES

RECOMMENDED WOOD TYPE: HICKORY WOOD

INGREDIENTS

- 2 cedar grilling planks
- 4 salmon fillets, skin on
- 2 tablespoons extra virgin olive oil
- 1 teaspoon fresh thyme, minced
- 1 tablespoon balsamic vinegar
- 2 teaspoons orange zest, grated
- ¼ cup honey
- ½ cup Dijon mustard
- Salt and pepper to taste

HOW TO

1. Place planks in pan and cover them with water, let them soak for an hour
2. Pre-heat your EGG to 400 degrees F and set it for direct cooking
3. Take a bowl and whisk in mustard, honey, orange zest, 1 teaspoon thyme, vinegar
4. Transfer planks on grids and lock lid, let them heat for 3 minutes
5. Open lid and turn planks over, brush with oil and add salmon fillets
6. Season with salt and pepper, brush will with your glaze
7. Cook for 12-15 minutes
8. Enjoy with a garnish with thyme

NUTRITION VALUES (PER SERVING)

- Calories: 335
- Fat: 20g
- Carbohydrates: 5g
- Protein: 31g

PERFECTLY SEARED UP TUNA

SERVING: 4

PREP TIME: 10 MINUTES

COOK TIME: 5-10 MINUTES

RECOMMENDED WOOD TYPE: HICKORY WOOD

INGREDIENTS

- 2 tablespoons sesame seeds, toasted
- 1 teaspoon sriracha
- ¼ cup honey
- ¼ cup pineapple juice
- 1 teaspoon corn starch
- ¼ cup soy sauce
- 2 ahi tuna steaks

How To

1. Pre-heat your EGG to 500 degrees F
2. Take a bowl and mix in cornstarch and soy sauce, and mix until smooth
3. Add pineapple juice, sriracha and honey
4. Place pot on your stove over medium heat, bring the mix to a boil
5. Lower down heat to low and simmer for 3-4 minutes, until it is thick
6. Remove heat
7. Add iron skillet to EGG and add oil, sear tuna steaks, making sure to brush with the mixture
8. Garnish and enjoy!

Nutrition Values (Per Serving)

- Calories: 364
- Fat: 16g
- Carbohydrates: 12g
- Protein: 40g

CHAPTER 7: GAME RECIPES

HEARTY CHERRY SMOKED VENISON LOIN

SERVING: 4

PREP TIME: 20 MINUTES

COOK TIME: 30 MINUTES

RECOMMENDED WOOD TYPE: CHERRY WOOD

INGREDIENTS

- 1 and ¼ pounds loin of venison
- Salt to taste
- Pinch of ground cumin
- 4 tablespoons almond oil
- 1 shallot, chopped
- 1 garlic clove, peeled
- 1 teaspoon pink peppercorn
- 1 teaspoon sesame seeds
- 4 courgettes, sliced
- 3 fresh lemons

HOW TO

1. Season venison with salt and pepper
2. Pre-heat your EGG to 300 degrees F and set it for direct cooking
3. Roast venison on grid, making sure to keep turning it for every 60-90 seconds, cook for 5-7 minutes
4. Take a pan and add oil, shallots, garlic, pink peppercorn, sesame seeds and heat for 30 seconds
5. Add courgettes and cook for 2 minutes on high heat
6. Drizzle lemon juice on top and serve with venison

NUTRITION VALUES (PER SERVING)

- Calories: 444
- Fat: 27g
- Carbohydrates: 6g
- Protein: 44g

CORNISH GAME HENS

SERVING: 4

PREP TIME: 20 MINUTES

COOK TIME: 2-3 HOURS

RECOMMENDED WOOD TYPE: APPLE WOOD

INGREDIENTS

- 2 Cornish Game hens
- Salt and pepper to taste
- 4 tablespoons butter
- 1 cup quick cooking seasoned brown rice
- 1 small onion, chopped
- ½ cup squeezed orange juice
- ½ cup apricot jelly

How To

1. Season the birds with salt and pepper
2. Take a small saucepan over low heat and add 2 tablespoon of butter, melt the butter and stir in rice and onion
3. Stuff the hens with the rice mix and secure the legs with twine
4. Rinse the saucepan and put it back to low heat
5. Melt remaining 2 tablespoon of butter and stir in orange juice alongside apricot jelly
6. Whisk until smooth
7. Baste the hen with the jelly glaze
8. Pre-heat your EGG to 275 degrees F and set it for in-direct cooking
9. Transfer to EGG and smoke for 2-3 hours until internal temperature reaches 170 degrees F
10. Brush with more jelly and enjoy!

Nutrition Values (Per Serving)

- Calories: 552
- Fat: 41g
- Carbohydrates: 10g
- Protein: 45g

SMOKED RABBIT

SERVING: 4

PREP TIME: 15 MINUTES + 60 MINUTES MARINATING TIME

COOK TIME: 2 HOURS

RECOMMENDED WOOD TYPE: APPLE WOOD

INGREDIENTS

- 1 piece of cottontail all skinned and gutted
- 2 tablespoon of Kosher Salt
- ½ a cup of white vinegar
- Water as needed

FOR THE RUB

- 1 tablespoon of garlic powder
- 1 tablespoon of cayenne pepper
- 1 tablespoon of salt
- 1 bottle of BBQ sauce

HOW TO

1. Take a bowl and pour in your kosher salt alongside the white vinegar to make your brine
2. Pour the brine over your rabbit using a shallow dish and add just enough water to cover up the whole of your rabbit
3. Let it sit for an hour
4. Pre-heat your smoker to a temperature of 200 degrees F
5. Take a bowl and whisk in the garlic powder, salt, pepper and cayenne pepper to make the rubbing
6. Season the rabbit nicely
7. Let it smoke for two hours and keep adding wood pellets after every 15 minutes
8. Remove the rabbit from your smoker and serve hot

NUTRITION VALUES (PER SERVING)

- Calories: 824
- Fat: 42g
- Carbohydrates: 35g
- Protein: 40g

CHAPTER 8: DESSERTS RECIPES

EASY DUMP CAKE

SERVING: 4

PREP TIME: 10 MINUTES

COOK TIME: 30-45 MINUTES

RECOMMENDED WOOD TYPE: HICKORY WOOD

INGREDIENTS

- 1 box cake mix of your choosing
- 2 cans of your desired pie filling
- 1 stick of butter

HOW TO

1. Pre-heat your EGG to 375 degrees F and set it indirect cooking
2. Spread the contents of the pie to the bottom of a pan, sprinkle cake mix on top
3. Melt butter in sauce pot and drizzle over cake mix
4. Transfer to the EGG and bake for about 45 minutes
5. Enjoy!

NUTRITION VALUES (PER SERVING)

- Calories: 328
- Fat: 9g
- Carbohydrates: 61g
- Protein: 2g

THE AWESOME CHEESECAKE

SERVING: 4

PREP TIME: 10 MINUTES

COOK TIME: 10 MINUTES

RECOMMENDED WOOD TYPE: HICKORY WOOD

INGREDIENTS

- 4 tablespoons unsalted butter
- 6 tablespoons all-purpose flour
- 1 cup milk
- 1 beer
- 2 teaspoons Dijon mustard
- 1 teaspoon garlic powder
- 1 teaspoon salt
- 1 teaspoon cayenne pepper
- 6 cups sharp cheddar cheese

HOW TO

1. Pre-heat your EGG to 400 degrees F
2. Take a large steel bowl and melt in butter, whisk in flour and mix well to make a roux
3. Place it over heat and slowly keep heating it until milky smooth
4. Add remaining ingredients to the bowl and transfer to EGG, cook for about 10 minutes until the cheese is completely smooth
5. Serve and enjoy!

NUTRITION VALUES (PER SERVING)

- Calories: 615
- Fat: 41g
- Carbohydrates: 56g
- Protein: 8g

HERBED CHEESE CRACKERS

SERVING: 4

PREP TIME: 10 MINUTES

COOK TIME: 15 MINUTES

RECOMMENDED WOOD TYPE: HICKORY WOOD

INGREDIENTS

- 1/3 cup olive oil
- 1 pack of ranch dressing mix
- 1 tablespoon dried dill
- 1 tablespoon garlic powder
- 1 tablespoon mix of dill and citrus
- 12 ounces box of Cheez-It Snack Crackers, Baked, Original
- 11 ounce box of Nabisco Saltin Crackers, Premium, Mini

How To

1. Pre-heat your EGG to 250 degrees F
2. Take a bowl and whisk in first four ingredients, divide in half
3. Drizzle half of the liquid over the cheese crackers in a large sized bowl
4. Spread the mixture over a round cooking grid and transfer to EGG, bake for 15 minutes, making sure to keep stirring it after every 5 minutes
5. Let it cool and repeat the mixture with saltines
6. Once they are cooled, toss both together and serve
7. Enjoy!

Nutrition Values (Per Serving)

- Calories: 398
- Fat: 23g
- Carbohydrates: 39g
- Protein: 9g

CHAPTER 9: THE BASICS OF BIG GREEN EGG

WHAT IS BIG GREEN EGG?

To put it simply, Big Green EGG is essentially the name of one of the most well known as prolific manufacturer of famous Kamado Styled Ceramic BBQ Charcoal Cookers. But here's there thing, there are certain features that makes their appliance exceptional from other similar appliances in the market!

Not only do Big GREEN EGG maintains the highest level of quality possible when choosing materials to build their EGGS, the EGGs themselves are extremely versatile and easy to use!

Just a single EGG can be used for direct, indirect grilling as well as smoking and baking! The culinary possibilities using this particular appliance are pretty much endless! And that is expanded even further if you add a bunch of accessories to the mix .

THE DIFFERENT SIZES BIG GREEN EGG

For those of you who are just planning on buying your very first Big Egg, you should be aware that there are a number of different sizes that are available for you to purchase. The following section should give you a small breakdown of the different sizes that are available to you.

- **Mini:** This model is the absolutely perfect for those individuals who want to carry it to a picnic or have a small home. This unit weighs about 36 pounds and has a grid diameter of 10 inches. It has the capacity to hold about 2 chicken breasts in one go.

- **MiniMax:** This particular model is also awesome for camping and small parties. It is easy to carry and comes with a nifty and sturdy grip. It weighs 90 pounds and has a diameter of 13 inches. It can hold a 12 pounds turkey in one go.

- **Small:** This is perfect for individuals who have a small sized balcony or as an additional Egg to another large Egg. It weighs about 80 pounds and has a diameter of 13 inches. It can cook a turkey of about 12 pounds. It is pretty portable and compatible with convEGGtor, half moon raised grid, round grill work and jalapeno grill rack.

- **Medium:** This model is ideal for couples and new small families. Most accessories are supported by this model and it weighs about 113 pounds. It sports a diameter of 15 inches and can accommodate a turkey of 18 pounds. Best accessories for this model would be cast iron cooking grid, grid cleaner, vertical chicken roaster etc.

- **Large:** This one the most optimal size for moderately large sized families and most gatherings. It supports most accessories as well and has a diameter of 18.25 inches with 162 pounds weight. It can hold a 20 pounds turkey and supports most accessories such as the deep dish aking stone, convEGG tore, v rack and so on.

- **X-Large:** This particular model is best suited for large families and large friend gatherins. It allows for many meals to be cooked at same time, in fact twelve racks of ribs and 24 burgers can be made in a single session. It weights about 219 pounds and has a grid diameter of 24 inches. It has the capacity to hold 20 pound turkeys and can be used with convEGGtor, pizza peel and baking stone.

- **XX-Large:** This is the largest one of the bunch! It is not only suitable for large family, but perfect for large parties and commercial usage, and therefore should be considered for catering groups or restaurants.

HOW DOES THE EGG WORK?

Despite being absolutely simple and easy to use, the Big Green Egg is actually a marriage of perfect culinary engineering that allows the Egg to reach perfect cooking temperature in minutes! The unique design of the Egg also allows for efficient air flow making the process of cooking even more satisfying.

The break it down, the Egg actually has 4 different parts that works in conjunction to create the perfect cooking experience.

- The bottom fire box has a Flow Draft Door that follows EGG's patented design, which allows for superb air flow. The door even allows you to control the amount of air entering the appliance and fire box, giving you greater control and flexibility.
- The second part is the Fire-Box itself that uses natural lump charcoal to do its magic!
- Next, we the "Ceramic" cooking chamber that is completely air tight. This feature allows it to retain most of the heat and helps to keep the food moist and tasty.
- And finally, the multi variable "Dual" function lid made out of metal further helps to control the flow of air, while allowing you to keep the device closed for greater smoking experience.

Asides from all of those, the EGG's temperature control mechanism allows you to bake, smoke or Grill using your EGG at precise temperatures. The EGG gives you total control over the temperature with an accuracy that stays with a few degrees of your desired temperature. The EGG will allow you to reach maximum temperatures of up to 750 degrees F, which is unmatched by most other indoor ovens.

You should also keep in mind that despite the high temperatures, the EGG is actually very safe to use as the ceramic surface doesn't get hot at all, and the actual source is finely protected within the ceramic fire box.

And if you wondering about creating a mess, then don't at all! As the EGG is crafted using professional grade materials that ensure that it doesn't lose its glaze even after prolonged periods of time.

The ash build up here is also minimal.

HANDY TIPS FOR YOUR JOURNEY

If this is your first time using the EGG, there are certain things that you should know about as they will help you to enjoy the early days of your Egg even more.

- When using a BIG GREEN EGG, always make sure to keep it on flat, leveled surface
- The EGG are designed to be used with a metal nest, ensuring a gap between the egg and the bottom to allow air flow. Even if you are not using a nest, make sure to set it up in such a way that the air flow does not get obstructed.
- Make sure to never keep your Egg on flammable surface
- Never leave the dome opened
- It case there are high-winds, it is highly advised that you keep a close look at your EGG while during the cooking session in order to prevent any mishaps
- When firing up your EGG for the first time, try to prevent the EGG from reaching temperatures higher than 350 degrees F, as it will help the gasket adhesive to cure
- Make sure to never use fluid lighter to light up your EGG. These chemicals will greatly alter the flavor of your food. Instead, try opting for BGE electric charcoal starter to light up your charcoals
- When you are moving your Egg, first make sure that your Egg is complete cool. Never try to move a warm/hot EGG as it might cause harm to you.
- When cooking at temperatures above 400 degrees F, try to ensure that you lift the lid about 1-2 inches prior to opening it up completely. This allows a little amount of heat to escape and prevent any self injury, this process is also known as "Burping"

CHAPTER 10: A LITTLE BIT ABOUT THE DIFFERENT KINDS OF COOKING TYPES

The Big Green Egg's are very well known all around the world for their versatility and inspiring flexibility that is offered, thanks to the brilliant design of its manufacturer. However, if you don't know what the different techniques are, then how you are going to use it right?

Well, this particular chapter is dedicated for all of your new comers out there who might want to get a basic idea of what can be achieved using the EGG.

Instead of making a mess and confusing with all the details, let me break the individual parts down into simple easy to understand sections.

First,

DIRECT GRILLING

When talking about direct grilling, we are basically placing the directly over fire and cooking it by exposing it to heat and flame.

It's pretty much the perfect way to cook chops, steaks, chicken breast, burgers, fillets, veggies and other simple and quick to cook foods.

Basically, foods that are just tender and have a thickness of less than 2 inch are perfect for grilling directly.

When you are grilling directly, you should know that it slowly sears the outer surface of your meat and forms a fine yet satisfying crust, keeping all the juices perfectly locked inside giving an amazing flavor.

In fact, the meticulously designed EGG ensures that you don't get any hot spots or flare ups too!

Keep in mind though, that for some food, you might need to start direct grilling at a high temperature and then lower down the heat as you go by.

INDIRECT GRILLING

When you are considering Indirect Grilling, you are essentially cooking the food using a drip pan or something similar to the convEGGtor, ensuring that the ingredient is not directly exposed to flame, but is rather cooked by heat produced at the bottom of the pan.

To be more scientific, the food is cooked via convection that allows heat to radiate from the coal and dome of the EGG.

This allows you to prepare rotisserie as well, as it allows the appliance rotisserie cooking as well.

SMOKING

Following the tradition, it is actually possible to Smoke meals using your EGG. Smoking using your EGG allows you to cook your meals slowly and infuse them with the smoky flavors of the wood that you are using. It allows you to slowly break down the tissues and make the meat very tender.

Smoking requires a long time, for some foods smoking is done in a matter of mere minutes while for others it might take hours upon hours.

The result however, would always be extremely satisfying, literally fall-off-the bone type meat with a combination of complex flavors generated by the smoke and spices that you use.

Aside from the usual meat though, using the EGG you can also smoke various other types of food such as nuts, veggies, cheese and even nuts.

The recommended temperature for smoking using the EGG falls somewhere around 225 degrees F to about 275 degrees F.

The perfectly designed dome of the EGG makes it easier for pit masters to adjust the openings that allows for Smoke cooking. Not only that, the brilliant design of the EGG also allows it to maintain a steady temperature for hours on end.

A particular accessory known as the "convEGGtor" is awesome when it comes to smoking as it helps to add a fine barrier between the direct heat of your flame and food, while allowing the smoke to circulate nicely around the meal.

BAKING

This is something that most people don't know about, but EGG actually allows you to use the EGG as a classical brick oven that allows you to use the EGG to make pies, biscuits, bread, pizza as so on.

With absolutely precise temperature controls and heat holding capacities, it is possible to turn the EGG into the perfect baking stone!

The DOME shape further helps to create a fine environment for baking while the material helps to draw the moisture and create extra-ordinary dishes!

CHAPTER 11: SMOKING TIPS

TYPES OF SMOKERS

ELECTRIC SMOKERS

The electric smoker is the best smoker because it is very simple to use. Just set it, put your food in it and leave the rest of the work to the smoker. There is nothing an electric smoker can't grill, be it seafood, poultry, meat, cheese or bread. It requires little attention unlike other smokers like filling water bin, lighting wood or charcoal and checking on fuel frequently. Yes, unlike traditional smoker, electric smoker just need 2 to 4 ounce of wood chips that turns out a delicious and flavorful smoky food. Furthermore, they maintain cooking temperature really well. On the other hand, it sleek and stylish look and small size make it appropriate if you are living in an apartment or condo. Due to their simpler functions and hassle-free cooking, the electric smoker is a good choice for beginner cooks who want to get started with smoking food.

GAS SMOKERS

Gas smokers or propane smoker are much like a gas grill using propane as a fuel. Therefore, the heat for cooking remains consistent and steady. Furthermore, gas smokers are as easy to use, just set the temperature and walk away. However, frequent checks need to be done to make sure fuel doesn't run out. It isn't a big issue but one should keep in mind. And the best part, a gas smoker can be used when there is no electricity or when you need an oven. A gas smoker can take up to cooking temperature to 450 degrees, making this smoker flexible to be used as an oven. Another fantastic feature of gas smoker is its portability so they can use anywhere. Just pack it and take it along with you on your camping trips or other outdoor adventures.

CHARCOAL SMOKERS

Nothing can beat the flavor charcoal gives to your food. Its best flavor just simply can't match with any other smoker flavor. Unfortunately, setting a charcoal smoker, tuning fuel, maintaining cooking temperature and checking food can be a pain and you might burn the food. Not to worry, these hassles of a charcoal smoker does go away with practice and experience. Therefore, a charcoal smoker suits perfectly for serious grillers and barbecue purist who want flavors.

PELLET SMOKERS

Pellet smokers are making a surge due to their best feature of a pallet of maintaining a consistent temperature. It contains an automated system to drop pallets which frees the cook to monitor fuel level. The addition of thermostat gives the user the complete control the cooking temperature and grilling of food under ideal condition. In addition, the smoking food uses the heat from hardwood which gives food a delicious flavor. The only downside of pallet smoker is their high cost between the ranges of $100 to %600.

TYPES OF SMOKER WOODS

Smoker wood is an important element which you need to decide correctly to cook a delicious smoked food. The reason is that smoker chips of woods impart different flavors on the food you are cooking in the smoker. Therefore, you should know which smoker wood should be used to create a delicious smoked food. Here is the lowdown of smoker woods and which food is best with them.

1- Alder: A lighter smoker wood with natural sweetness.
Best to smoke: Any fish especially salmon, poultry and game birds.

2- Maple: This smoker wood has a mild and sweet flavor. In addition, its sweet smoke gives the food a dark appearance. For better flavor, use it as a combination with alder, apple or oak smoker woods.
Best to smoke: Vegetables, cheese, and poultry.

3- Apple: A mild fruity flavor smoker wood with natural sweetness. When mixed with oak smoker wood, it gives a great flavor to food. Let food smoke for several hours as the smoke takes a while to permeate the food with the flavors.
Best to smoke: Poultry, beef, pork, lamb, and seafood.

4- Cherry: This smoker wood is an all-purpose fruity flavor wood for any type of meat. Its smoke gives the food a rich, mahogany color. Try smoking by mixing it with alder, oak, pecan and hickory smoker wood.
Best to smoke: Chicken, turkey, ham, pork, and beef.

5- Oak: Oakwood gives a medium flavor to food which is stronger compared to apple wood and cherry wood and lighter compared to hickory. This versatile smoker wood works well blended with hickory, apple, and cherry woods.
Best to smoke: Sausages, brisket, and lamb.

6- Peach and Pear: Both smoker woods are similar to each other. They give food a subtle light and fruity flavor with the addition of natural sweetness.
Best to smoke: Poultry, pork and game birds.

7- Hickory: Hickory wood infuses a strong sweet and bacon flavor into the food, especially meat cuts. Don't over smoke with this wood as it can turn the taste of food bitter.

Best to smoke: Red meat, poultry, pork shoulder, ribs.

8- Pecan: This sweet smoker wood lends the food a rich and nutty flavor. Use it with Mesquite wood to balance its sweetness.
Best to smoke: Poultry, pork.

9- Walnut: This strong flavored smoker wood is often used as a mixing wood due to its slightly bitter flavor. Use walnut wood with lighter smoke woods like pecan wood or apple wood.
Best to smoke: Red meat and game birds.

10-Grape: Grape wood chips give a sweet berry flavor to food. It's best to use these wood chips with apple wood chips.
Best to smoke: Poultry

11- Mulberry: Mulberry wood chips is similar to apple wood chips. It adds natural sweetness and gives berry finish to the food.
Best to smoke: Ham and Chicken.

12-Mesquite: Mesquite wood chips flavor is earthy and slightly harsh and bitter. It burns fast and strongly hot. Therefore, don't use it for longer grilling.

Best to smoke: Red meat, dark meat.

THE DIFFERENT TYPES OF CHARCOAL AND THEIR BENEFITS

Charcoal is one of the efficient fuels for smoking. It burns hot, with more concentrated fire. Smoking food with charcoal is awesome. Though lighting charcoals, regulating airflows and controlling the heat is always a challenge, however, the excellent taste of food is worth this challenge. But, keep in mind that not all charcoals are equal and selecting one is a matter of preference.

LUMP CHARCOAL:

Lump charcoal or hardwood is the first choice of griller as a better fuel source. It is basically made by burning wood logs in an underground pit for a few days. As a result, water, sap, and other substances in log burn out, leaving behind a pure char or lump charcoal. This charcoal burns pure, hot and efficiently. They burn hotter in the beginner and burn cooler by the end. Therefore, lump charcoal is a good choice for broiling quickly or searing food at intense heat. In addition, the lump char also add the aroma of wood smoke into the food which takes the taste to another level of gastronomical heaven. Since, lump charcoal cool its fire in 30 minutes, replenish fire to maintain the temperature which takes only 5 to 10 minutes by adding few unlit coals. It's recommended to use lump charcoal with a combination of wood chips like maple, oak or hickory and refuel this wood chips every 40 minutes during smoking food.

CHARCOAL BRIQUETTES:

Charcoal briquettes are actually crushed charcoal. The major benefit of using this natural charcoal is its even shape and size. This is done by adding chemical binders and fillers like coal dust and compressing into a pillow shape. Therefore, creating a bed of coals is very easy with charcoal briquettes which are quite hard with uneven and irregular charcoals. The only downside is that they burn very quickly, more than lump charcoal. This creates a short window for smoking food, therefore, more briquettes need to add during grilling.

THE DIFFERENCE BETWEEN BARBECUING A MEAT AND SMOKING IT?

There are two main ways to cook meat that has become an increasingly popular cooking method: smoking or barbecuing. They are both different and require different cooking equipment, temperature, and timing. Following is the full comparison between smoking and barbecue.

BARBECUING MEAT:

Barbecue is a slow cooking, indirectly over low heat between 200 to 250 degrees F. Therefore, it is best suited for beef brisket, whole pig, turkeys or pork shoulder. These animals tend to have tough muscles which need slow cooking over low heat to get a moist and tender meat. It turns out an extremely tender and flavorful meat. The best example of a perfect barbecue is falling of meat off the bones. During the barbecue, the fuel needs to be filled frequently but do this quickly, as lifting lid of burner exposes meat to air which can turn it dry.

For barbecuing meat, the grill needs to be preheated until hot. For this light enough charcoals or bкisquettes so that their fire turns down for cooking. In the meantime, season meat and then when grill reaches to perfect cooking temperature, place seasoned meat on it. Having grill on perfect temperature is essential as meat won't stick to grilling grate.

Equipment: Fire pit, grill or a charcoal burner with lid.

Fueling: Lump wood charcoal, charcoal briquettes or wood chips combination like apple. Cherry and oak wood chips.

Best to smoke: A big cut of meats like Briskets, whole chicken, sausages, jerky, pork, and ribs.

Temperature: 190 to 300 degrees F

Timing: 2 hours to a day long.

SMOKING MEAT:

Smoking is one of the oldest cooking technique dating back to the first people living in caves. It was traditionally a food preservation method and with the time, its popularity never died. Smoking is a related process of barbecue. It's the best cooking method to bring out the rich and deep flavor of meat that tastes heavenly when meat is smoked until it comes off the bone.

During smoking, food is cooked below 200 degrees F cooking temperature. Therefore, smoking food requires a lot of time and patience. It infuses woody flavor into the meat and turns a silky and fall-of-bone meat. There are three ways to smoke food, cold smoke, hot smoke and adding liquid smoke. In these three types of smoking methods, liquid smoke is becoming increasingly common. Its main advantage is that smoke flavor is controlled. In addition, the effect of liquid smoke on meat is immediate.

There is another smoking method which called water smoking. It uses water smoker which is specifically designed to incorporate water in the smoking process. The water helps in controlling the temperature of smoker which is great for large cut meats for long hours.

Equipment: A closed container or high-tech smoker.

Fueling: The container will need an external source for a smoke. Wood chips are burn to add smoky flavor to the meat. However, the frequent check should be made to monitor and adjust temperature for smoking.

Best to smoke: A big cut of meats like Briskets, whole chicken, pork, and ribs.

Temperature: 68 to 176 degrees F

Timing: 1 hour to 2 weeks

THE CORE DIFFERENCE BETWEEN COLD AND HOT SMOKING

There are two ways to smoke meat that is cold smoking and hot smoking. In cold smoking, meat is cooked between 68 to 86 degrees F until smoked but moist. It is a good choice to smoke meat like chicken breast, steak, beef, pork chops, salmon, and cheese. The cold smoking concern with adding flavor to the meat rather than cooking. Therefore, when the meat is cold smoked, it should be cured, baked or steamed before serving.

On the other hand, hot smoking cooks the meat completely, in addition, to enhance its flavor. Therefore, meat should be a cook until its internal temperature is between 126 to 176 degrees F. Don't let meat temperature reach 185 degrees F as at this temperature, meat shrinks or buckles. Large meat cuts like brisket, ham, ribs and pulled pork turns out great when hot smoked.

THE CORE ELEMENTS OF SMOKING

There are six essential elements of smoking.

1. Wood chips: Chip of woods are used as a fuel either alone or in combination with charcoals. In addition, these chips add fantastic flavor to the meat. Therefore, chips of wood should only be used which suits best to the meat.

2. Smoker: There are basically four choices from which a smoker should be the pick. The choices are an electric smoker, charcoal smoker, gas smoker and pellet smoker. Each has its own advantages and downsides.

3. Smoking time: Smoking time is essential for perfect of meat cuts. It is actually the time when the internal temperature reaches its desired values. It may take 2 hours up to more than two weeks.

4. Meat: The star of the show is meat that needs to be more tender, juicy and flavorful after smoking. Make sure, the meat you sure has fat trimmed from it. In addition, it should complement the wood of chips.

5. Rub: Rubs, mixture or salt and spices, add sweetness and heat to the meat. They should be prepared in such a way that all types of flavor should be balanced in the meat.

6. Mops: Mops or liquid is often used during smoking meat. It adds a little bit flavor to the meat and maintains tenderness and moisture throughout the smoking process.

THE BASIC PREPARATIONS FOR SMOKING MEAT

CHOOSING SMOKER

The major and foremost step is to choose a smoker. You can invest in any type of the smoker: charcoal smoker, gas smoker or an electric smoker. A charcoal smoker runs for a long time and maintain steadier heat in the smoker and give meat pure flavors. A good choice for beginner cook for smoking meat is a gas smoker where there is no need to monitor temperature but it comes with a downside that meat won't have much flavor compared to charcoal. On the other hand, the simplest, easiest and popular smoker is an electric smoker. Cooking with electric smoker involves only two-step: turn it on, put meat in it and walk away. Read more details about smokers in the section "type of smokers".

CHOOSING FUEL

Wood chips add a unique flavor to the meat, therefore, select that wood chips that would enhance the taste of meat. Some wood of chips have a stronger flavor, some have mild while others are just enough to be alone for smoking. Check out the section titled "types of smoker wood" to get to know and decide chips of wood that will complement your meat.

TYPE OF SMOKING METHOD

You have two choices to smoke meat, either using wet smoking, dry smoking, liquid smoke or water smoking. Read the section "The core difference between cold and hot smoking" to find out differences between each. In addition, go through smoking meat portion in the section "the difference between barbecuing a meat and smoking it".

SOAKING CHIPS OF WOOD

Wood chips need to soak in order to last longer for fueling smoking. The reason is dry wood that burns quickly and this means, adding fuel to the smoker which can result in dry smoked meat. There isn't any need of using wood chips when smoking for a shorter time. Prepare wood chips by soaking them in water for at least 4 hours before starting smoking. Then drain chips and wrap and seal them in an aluminium foil. Use toothpick or fork for poking holes into the wood chips bag.

SET SMOKER

Each type of smoker have its own way to start smoking. For wood or charcoal smoker, first, light up half of the charcoals and wait until their flame goes down. Then add remaining charcoal and wood chips if using. Wait they are lighted and giving heat completely, then push charcoal aside and place meat on the other side of grilling grate. This is done to make sure that meat is indirectly smoked over low heat. Continue adding charcoal and/or soaked wood chips into the smoker.

For gas/propane or electric smoker, just turn it on according to manufacturer guideline and then add soaked wood chips into chip holder and fill water receptacle if a smoker has one. Either make use of the incorporated thermostat or buy your own to monitor the internal temperature of the smoker. When smoker reaches to desired preheated temperature, add meat to it.

SELECTING MEAT FOR SMOKING

Choose the type of meat which tastes good with a smoky flavor. Following meat goes well for smoking.

Beef: ribs, brisket and corned beef.

Pork: spare ribs, roast, shoulder, and ham.

Poultry: whole chicken, whole turkey, and big game hens.

Seafood: Salmon, scallops, trout, and lobster.

GETTING MEAT READY

Prepare meat according to the recipe. Sometimes meat is cured, marinated or simply seasoned with the rub. These preparation methods ensure smoked meat turn out flavorful, tender and extremely juicy.

Brine is a solution to treating poultry, pork or ham. It involves dissolving brine ingredients in water poured into a huge container and then adding meat to it. Then let soak for at least 8 hours and after that, rinse it well and pat dry before you begin smoking.

Marinate treat beef or briskets and add flavors to it. It's better to make deep cuts in meat to let marinate ingredients deep into it. Drain meat or smoke it straightaway.

Rubs are commonly used to treat beef, poultry or ribs. They are actually a combination of salt and many spices, rubbed generously all over the meat. Then the meat is left to rest for at least 2 hours or more before smoking it.

Before smoking meat, make sure it is at room temperature. This ensures meat is cooked evenly and reach its internal temperature at the end of smoking time.

PLACING MEAT INTO THE SMOKER

Don't place the meat directly over heat into the smoker because the main purpose of smoking is cooking meat at low temperature. Set aside your fuel on one side of the smoker and place meat on the other side and let cook.

Smoking time: The smoking time of meat depends on the internal temperature. For this, use a meat thermometer and insert it into the thickest part of the meat. The smoking time also varies with the size of meat. Check recipes to determine the exact smoking time for the meat.

BASTING MEAT

Some recipes call for brushing meat with thin solutions, sauces or marinade. This step not only makes meat better in taste, it also helps to maintain moisture in meat through the smoking process. Read recipe to check out if basting is necessary.

Taking out meat: When the meat reaches its desired internal temperature, remove it from the smoker. Generally, poultry should be removed from smoker when its internal temperature reaches to 165 degrees F. For ground meats, ham, and pork, the internal temperature should be 160 degrees F. 145 degrees F is the internal temperature for chops, roast, and steaks.

CONCLUSION

As you can see from these recipes, the world of smoking is only as limited as your imagination! Sweet, savory, vegetable, mineral, meat- you can smoke almost anything. As you get more comfortable with these recipes, feel free to start experimenting on your own. The basic principles hold true, but your own taste buds can drive you. Good luck, and happy smoking!

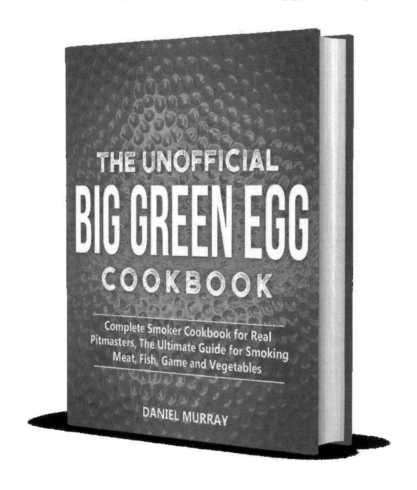

GET YOUR FREE GIFT

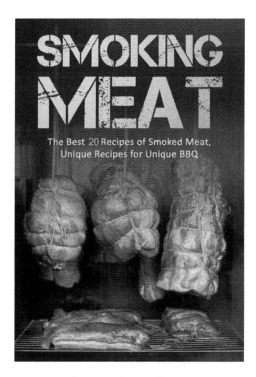

Subscribe to our Mail List and get your FREE copy of the book

'Smoking Meat: The Best 20 Recipes of Smoked Meat, Unique Recipes for Unique BBQ'

https://tiny.cc/smoke20

OTHER BOOKS BY DANIEL MURRAY

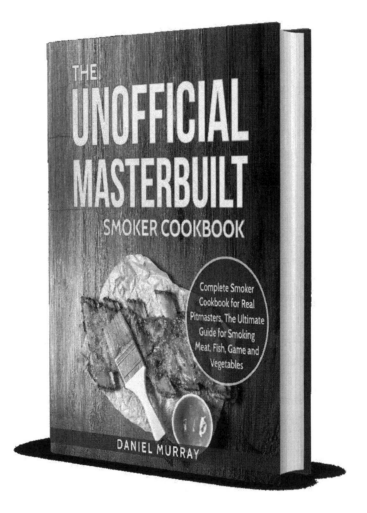

https://www.amazon.com/qp/product/B07JVHZ4PJ

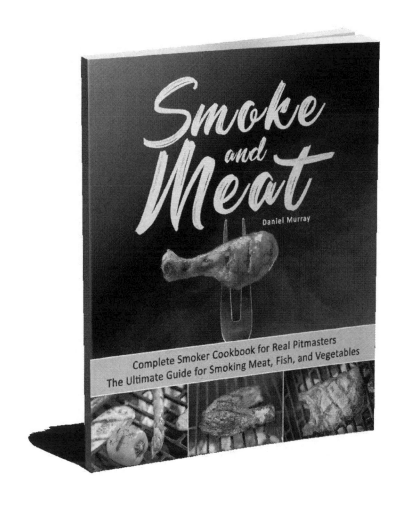

https://www.amazon.com/dp/B07D8NFZ3F

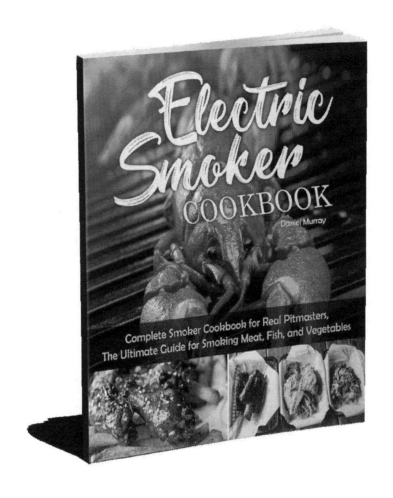

HTTPS://WWW.AMAZON.COM/DP/B07DKZ3NSK

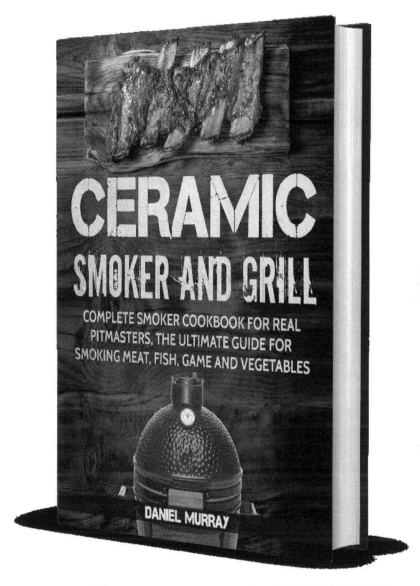

HTTPS://WWW.AMAZON.COM/DP/B07GSKRLB8

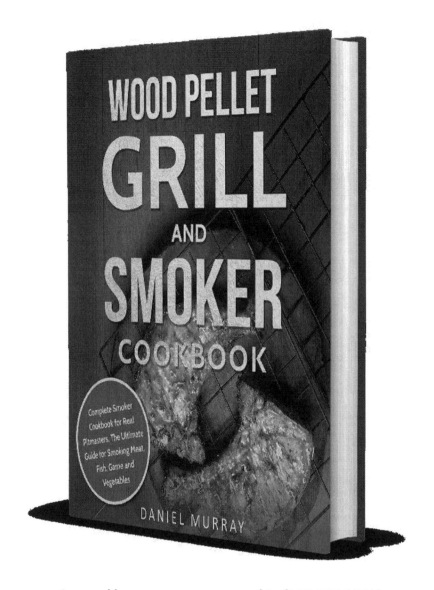

https://www.amazon.com/dp/173158654X